14/07/23

C000262824

Kaz Cooke

PENGUIN BOOKS

PENGUIN BOOKS

Published by the Penguin Group
Penguin Group (Australia)
250 Camberwell Road, Camberwell, Victoria 3124, Australia
(a division of Pearson Australia Group Pty Ltd)
Penguin Group (NZ)
Cnr Airborne and Rosedale Roads, Albany, Auckland, New Zealand
(a division of Pearson New Zealand Ltd)

Penguin Books Ltd, Registered Offices: 80 Strand, London WC2R 0RL, England

First published by Penguin Books Australia Ltd 1996
21 23 25 27 26 24 22

Text and illustrations copyright © Kaz Cooke, 1996

All rights reserved. Without limiting the rights under copyright reserved above, no
part of this publication may be reproduced, stored in or introduced into a retrieval
system, or transmitted, in any form or by any means (electronic, mechanical,
photocopying, recording or otherwise), without the prior written permission of both
the copyright owner and the above publisher of this book.

Typeset in 10pt Futura by Midland Typesetters, Maryborough, Victoria
Printed and bound in Australia by McPherson's Printing Group, Maryborough,
Victoria

National Library of Australia
Cataloguing-in-Publication data

Cooke, Kaz, 1962– .
The little book of stress.
ISBN 0 14 026620 8.
1. Stress (Psychology) – Humor. 2. Affirmations – Humor.
I. Title.
155.90420207

www.penguin.com.au

'He who letteth the tribulations meander past his door, he who speaketh only of flowing serenities, he who seemeth to become one with his unconscious mind, in repose from morn 'til night. Who he? A complete idiot.'

Dhagi Shri Dalai Glenys Heather Thud

intro

I don't know about you, but all those little books of deadly-serious, one-thought-per-page, calm-down-this-second, hippy-drippy nonsense make me really tense. After all, who's more likely to get along in life: the wafty hippy idiot, or the person who can handle some of life's stressful realities? It seems to be time for *The Little Book of Stress*.

Follow the recommendations in this book and you will be very practised at all of life's most angst-ridden moments. You'd also be stark raving bonkers. To be perfectly frank, these suggestions are like camouflage-print novelty condoms: **you're not meant to actually TRY them**. And remember, if you really want to be calm, just reverse all the suggestions.

(Oh *all right*, I'll admit it. I wrote this book because, like most authors, I had a tacky ambition to write a book with only one thought per page. Thank you.)

flip ▶ ▶ ▶

Never sit if you can stand, walk if you can run, breathe if you can hyperventilate.

Have you ever noticed how long grass bends before the wind, ensuring it doesn't break under the pressure; rippling and bowing in the breeze, going with the flow? Stupid, isn't it?

If you're on a picnic, watch out for European wasps.

Gardening: that yard is full of thorns and poisonous thingies. Get a noisy weed whacker and lay into it. With a bit of luck, it may lead to another fight with the neighbours.

Reaffirm your faith in fantasy:
believe in guardian angels and
beautiful wee fairies at the bottom
of your garden. Then remember
you've killed them all with a
weed whacker.

If you are angered by something,
fire off a vicious and threatening
fax in the heat of the moment.
People will appreciate having
it in writing.

If your neighbours annoy you,
shout at them.

Have a baby, move house and
get divorced at the same time.
You might also like to begin a new
job and come out of the closet,
just to get everything over
and done with at once.

Shop and eat at places with really bad service.

Communicate by whingeing, shouting and using aggressive gestures. This will clear a room in no time and leave you in control. Being in control, even of an empty room, is terribly impressive.

Write down a list of all your most
intimate worries. Chant the list
hourly until you become
unconscious or rigid with horror.

When speaking at a meeting,
imagine that everyone sees you
completely naked, or dressed only
in baggy, grey Y-fronts.

Try to do something about decreased funding to hospitals and schools.

Aromatherapy: throw some
stinkweed into a hot bath. This will
force you to leave the house and
think of something useful to do.

Always drive in the city at peak hour, and sound your horn almost constantly.

If you are trying to cut down on sunflower seeds, nuts and alfalfa, take up smoking, drinking and doing drugs. It will really help.

Bolt your food.
Anybody who thinks you should
chew every mouthful thirty-two
times hasn't got enough to do.

Brew yourself a relaxing tea made from shredded cabbage, rotten orange peel and old twigs. Now just throw it over somebody you don't like.

When ordering a taxi, request a raving, right-wing rude driver with B.O. who listens to raving, right-wing radio and doesn't believe in red lights.

Make your own meditation tape
using music and the sounds of
nature: heavy metal, hyena roars,
crocodile rattles and the noise of
vicious aardvark attacks.

Take up parachuting, caving, psychotherapy and smoking in the same week.

Begin each day with three long blacks, a Coke and a packet of Peter Stuyvesant.

Watch the news.

Every freckle might be a melanoma,
every throat clearing could be lung
cancer and a headache might
mean a brain tumour. (An itchy toe
often heralds a sudden
leg amputation.)

If you're feeling too relaxed, tighten
up every part of your body slowly.
Now, hold.

Picture calm rainforests and
beaches. Now wonder when the
woodchippers, property developers
and nuclear bomb testers will
be arriving.

Strap a first aid kit to the back of
your head in case of an emergency.

Wear white, which in theory is calming but in practice means you spend every waking hour either trying not to drop a pikelet down your front, or developing a personal relationship with the washing machine.

Try to be the centre of attention at all times. If necessary, break the furniture.

Posture is important.
Always pretend you've got a
broomstick up your pooter.

Wear high heels.

Watch animal documentaries – particularly ones showing animals eating their own young, trying to kill each other after sex, males fighting to the death, and anything to do with vultures.

Change the way you look at things.
Come to think of it, don't look at
things at all – try denial.

Explore your dreams. Interesting results can be obtained through too much rich food, psychotropic drugs and repressed thoughts. Remember – your dreams are to be taken strictly literally.

Discover your inner child – it's probably freaked out, needs to go pee and wants to know if you're nearly there yet.

It is vital that you look as glamorous as possible at all times. Get up an hour early each morning for plucking, waxing, make-up, hair-wrangling and clothes selection. This goes for women too.

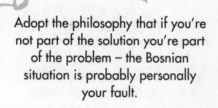

Adopt the philosophy that if you're
not part of the solution you're part
of the problem – the Bosnian
situation is probably personally
your fault.

Practise frowning and sneering.
These expressions take more muscle
work than smiling and will therefore
give your face a good work-out.

Volunteer to be the sexual harassment counsellor at your workplace.

Try to be funny all the time.
Everyone likes a laugh, so make
sure you slip a pun into every
sentence. If nobody laughs,
try two or three puns.

Put each sock in a different drawer.
This will present more of a
challenge when you're
late for work.

Sit peacefully in a church and think of church history: witchburning perhaps, or child abuse, genocide, the amassing of disgusting wealth, the repression of women, inquisitions, castrating child choir singers, the denial of Santa Claus and the support of fascists in power.

Taunt a religious fanatic.

File things under the seventh letter of their name. For example, 'Correspondence' would be filed under 'P'. This makes for interesting retrieval and will keep everybody alert.

Wear unnatural fabrics and wildly
roll around on nylon carpets.

Weigh every sliver of food which passes your lips and furtively catalogue it in a small notebook.

Enjoy a sunset up until the point you
realise the colours are caused by
airborne pollutants.

Never forget that everything you touch is covered with about sixty-seven trillion totally disgusting dust mites and they all look like microscopic, slavering rhinocerousy monsters.

Organise your own wedding with special attention to the needs of any mothers-in-law involved.

Keep your diary on small scraps of brown paper bag, secure only in the knowledge that you're probably supposed to be somewhere else right now.

Public speaking engagement?
Get drunk beforehand and wing it.

Pets are an important part of mental health. Buy a boa constrictor and let it roam free. It can fling itself at you from the rafters at random intervals.

Tell so many lies you can't remember to whom you told what.

To engender a spirit of challenge, keep your house key in a bucket of similar unmarked keys next to your front door.

Drop off to sleep by trying to identify your neighbours' cars by the sound of the car alarms you set off just before retiring.

A rested person is a complacent person. Set your alarm to go off every hour through the night. (People with children may skip this page.)

Stay alert about your body image
and encourage weight loss by
wearing underpants that are two
sizes too small, and back to front.

If you are relaxing in a large, warm bubble bath, just think of the natural resources you're wasting. In the shower, think of the film *Psycho*.

Stay away from waves.

You should have two mobile phones, a home phone and fax, a work phone and fax and a minimum of one paging service, three email addresses, a communications satellite and two cans joined by a piece of string. Make sure everybody has all of your numbers.

Diet pills are a great shortcut to feeling paranoid, itchy and furious.

If you need a bit of a lift, rub some Tiger Balm on your genitals. This will cause screaming, which will help keep you awake.

To make sure you don't miss any callers, install a siren and flashing light instead of a doorbell.

Test out Neighbourhood Watch in your area. Next time you go away, leave the front door open. Have a good holiday.

Lie awake at night in case an
axe-murderer breaks in.

Make a list of things you are not allowed to think about. Post a copy to yourself every Thursday.

Never ignore a ringing telephone.
Maybe somebody died.

Make a list of all your most
embarrassing moments.
Send the list to a local radio
station for broadcast.

Plan a holiday in a war zone.

Spend time with people who are calm and smiling no matter what happens. Their stupidity will send your blood pressure through the ceiling.

Get some more credit cards.

Fix any electrical problems yourself.
All you need is a good pair of
pliers, some gaffer tape, metal-
soled shoes and life insurance.

Get on the Internet and agree to marry a total stranger from another hemisphere.

Experiment with the social fabric.
Go to a football club end-of-season
celebration and shout, 'You are all
POOFTERS!'.

Try using the cat as a pillow.

Get a contract signed straight
away. You'll have more time,
and reason, to worry about the
fine print later.

Treat every day as if it were
Monday morning.

Burn relaxing candles and incense all around the house. This will set off the smoke alarm and create a vibrant soundscape art happening, especially when the fire brigade arrives.

Act young, wild and free – park in
a no-standing zone.

Young children can show us the way to uninhibited happiness. Cook with them to discover the joy of uninhibited frenzied mess-creating and burn opportunities.

Use plenty of spray insecticides,
and then read the label.

Darkness is very soothing until you bark your shins on the furniture and stand on unidentifiable, squishy things.

Walking in the rain can be very carefree, until you realise you could get triple pneumonia.

Commune with climatic possibilities.
Go and stand outside on a windy
day. After a couple of hours you'll
feel suitably shifty and agitated.

Have several aliases or several jobs. Better still, combine both cunning plans.

Save space by throwing away all your receipts and then simply mentally reconstruct them at the end of each tax year.

A couple of coffees before bed at night with a nice sugar bun won't do you any harm.

Try not to fart.

Sleep in your contact lenses, on hessian sheets.

Use public transport.

Use the road system.

Cultivate an air of authority by
making yourself completely
indispensable, and believing that if
you're not at every meeting and
every decision your head might
actually explode.

Shave your eyebrows off and draw
them on each morning.

Many foods – such as alfalfa, tofu and, oh, toucan toenails – are said to enhance a feeling of relaxation, but they all taste like crap and you can't get them at the local hamburger shop, so why bother?

Make hard and fast rules for yourself. Punish yourself if you break them.

The sea is so peaceful, yet challenging. Try solo-yachting from the Antarctic to Africa with a small compass and a cut lunch.

Marry an alcoholic.

Space is beautiful. Stare at the velvety expanse of stars and wonder which one might be an enormous meteor on a collision course with Earth.

Eat a *lot* of licorice on a first date.

Try hard to make niceness your
byword, no matter how many
people walk all over you.
Just keep your simmering
resentment to yourself.

Don't be afraid to set yourself unrealistic goals: it will be so much more challenging.

Nobody ever takes notice of a meek person. Use a loud, strident voice at all times. If someone does not understand, for example a foreigner, talk louder.

If you ever feel overwhelmed by life,
take your mind off it by beginning
some home renovations.

To encourage self-expression, give children educational musical toys with loud, discordant noises.

If you have children, attach homing devices to their ears.

Try to enliven your world by telling everybody what you really think of them and encourage them to do the same to you.

Don't spread yourself too thinly –
choose one of your problems and
obsess about it.

If you carry a handbag make sure it has a dark interior and holds about three kilos of random stuff. This makes finding what you need an exciting prospect. The same applies to bulging pockets, toolboxes and car boots.

Rubber or sandpaper underwear
can help keep you alert.

Tell yourself that if you're late for work, everybody you know will turn against you, the sky will darken, and demons will come to earth with strange winged beasties and put an eternal curse on you and your descendants.

Become more candid. Confess every indiscretion you have kept hidden for years, and tell your partner and family.

While single, remind yourself of coupledom by playing a sleep-defying tape of snoring and other offensive night noises.

Invite a new love interest to dinner
and cook something you have never
heard of before, from a cookbook
in the original French.

If your pants are too tight after a large meal, go to the casualty section of the nearest teaching hospital. Massive food poisoning should be ruled out.

Try to spark up a long-term
relationship by dropping hints that
you might be having an affair.

Go to a very groovy, young hairstylist who usually gets home at 4 am and say, 'Just do whatever you like, I need a change, just something different'.

Pay attention to all five food groups: fruit, sausage rolls, popcorn, custard tarts and lunch.

Play chicken.

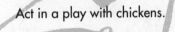

Act in a play with chickens.

Whenever you are dancing,
consider that there are probably
more attractive people than you
judging your technique.

Employ opera singers to give you
the weather report.

If you need something quickly, speed up your words so that they run together. Squeaking in a high-pitched way usually gets attention more quickly than a mellifluous request.

Many people grind their teeth
unconsciously at night, but there's
no reason why you can't do it
knowingly in the daytime.

Whenever there is a delay, use the time constructively on exercise (pacing up and down), grooming (pulling your hair) and management training (shouting at junior staff members).

Passionate personal relationships
are vivid and exciting, and shouting
and insulting each other all day
exercises the uvula muscle no end.

Old-fashioned party games can be fun. See how many chocolate biscuits you can eat in a row without throwing up. Blindfolded, see if you can find the toilet fast enough.

Eat restaurant meals as quickly as possible in case you are called away unexpectedly.

Exercise is a known cause of sweating. Avoid this by getting right under your bed and refusing any requests to come out.

Read a psychiatric dictionary and, just for fun, try to see how many of your character traits match up with conditions in the book.

If involved in a romantic clinch, maintain mind control. This is a good time to reflect on the size of your thighs, or how fast you're going bald.

Enjoy nature rambles, paying particular attention to the few, tragic, remaining examples of indigenous flora. Identify the fauna closest to extinction.

When doodling in a meeting,
make sure that every single doodle
means something, has artistic
merit and can be explained,
analysed and exhibited.

According to some cultures, if our hair or fingernail clippings fall into the wrong hands, curses can be put on us. Where are your clippings?

Don't save your best clothes for special occasions. Wear them every day for effect. It might be fun to wear high heels to a farm, or a silk suit to the site inspection.

If you disagree with somebody,
make your feelings known.
Use positive reinforcement, such as:
'You still wouldn't have a clue,
would you?'.

Every day take some time to sit
at your desk, breathe deeply and
say to yourself:
'Have I left the iron on?'.

Carry a gun.

Here's a good exercise. Place your head between your knees, cover your face with your hands and rock back and forth slowly, chanting, 'Oh my God'.

Practise harsh, shallow breathing.

Keep up your circulation by striding
and stomping around. Wave your
hands violently above your head
like a windmill.

Tell everyone at work you're in therapy. Preferably announce this during a meeting.

Have a video night in. Try *Alien*, *Aliens*, *The Birds* or any other Hitchcock films, and anything with 'Friday the 13th' in its title.

Try for 'closure' in your life. Contact people in your past and rake over old, hurtful incidents.

Play hard. There are opportunities for cheating or crying foul even in a game of Snap with small children.

Invite all your ex-lovers to the same party.

Help a humanitarian agency clear
land mines (manufactured in the
first world) in a third world country.

Share your problems, and then wonder whether everyone thinks you're neurotic or incompetent.

Save money. Queue all night
and shop at the annual department
store rioting sales.

Test your reflexes. Get into a sealed bag with a rabid ferret.

Hurry.

Worry.

Many naturopaths suggest Bach Flower Rescue Remedy for stressful moments, but it's probably easier to get a bottle of tequila at short notice.

Leave all your Christmas shopping
until 24 December.

about the author

Kaz Cooke is a writer and cartoonist who tires of loose talk about Reiki healing, flabbity New Age thinking and other passive, witless hippy crap. She is driven to a frenzy by the rude insistence of the feral calm movement that everybody should behave like a crash test dummy in order to attain serenity. She believes that completely calm people ought to be slapped (just to check if they're conscious). Kaz does yoga once a year.

◀◀◀ flip